THE VARIETIES OF EARTH-CENTRED PRACTICES

GreenSpirit book series

The Varieties of EARTH-CENTRED PRACTICES

Eight Green Ways

Edited by Santoshan (Stephen Wollaston)

GreenSpirit

**GreenSpirit is a registered charity based in the UK.
The main contents/written material, editing, design and promotional work for our GreenSpirit Book Series is done on a purely voluntary basis or given freely by contributors who share our passion for Gaia-centred spirituality.**

Published by GreenSpirit
137 Ham Park Road, London E7 9LE
www.greenspirit.org.uk
Registered Charity No. 1045532

Low-cost eBook editions in various formats are also available.

Design and artwork by Santoshan (Stephen Wollaston).
Front cover and title page photo by StockSnap, from Pixabay.com.

Contents

Introduction

Let us accept all the different paths as different rivers running toward the same ocean.
~ Swami Satchidananda

This book brings together a collection of especially commissioned articles by contemporary and former trustees of GreenSpirit. My reason for compiling it has been to highlight disparate paths that can be seen as *green* although like any topic there is always more that could be included.

When I suggested the theme for a new title in the GreenSpirit Book Series, the idea was received positively by members of GreenSpirit's publications team. Finding the right people to write for each chapter was also straightforward, as they are all people I know from my involvement in the charity, and to whom I wish to give a personal thanks for well-crafted and knowledgeable contributions. Biographies about the authors are listed at the back of this book.

Overall, what I find encouraging in each person's

writings is their passion for the areas they wrote on. Whilst compiling and editing, I noticed there was at times an overlap of themes, yet by having different writers with dissimilar backgrounds highlighted each person's distinct understanding of things they wrote about, which, for me, has made for a wonderful synthesis of ideas and practices.

Summary of the Chapters

In the opening chapter, Marian Van Eyk McCain, who has written and published much over the years on simplicity, self-sufficiency, and downshifting, draws on her many years of wisdom and her experience of living simply. She informs us how opting for simplicity helped her life to become fuller, richer and more enjoyable. She also reminds us that simplicity doesn't necessarily mean having less to do, as it may in fact require more planning, more thinking about, and a lot more effort to live than the average mainstream lifestyle that the majority of people live in today's world.

In the following chapter, Ian Mowll writes about the power of shared stories and how they can motivate us to pursue healthier goals and transform restrictive patterns. Since early history, Ian informs us, stories have helped orientate people on their life journeys and united people together. He writes how the discovery and knowledge of galaxies, the Big Bang and evolution theory have become a new creation story that is particularly relevant for our times – what is often called "the New Universe Story" – that can supply us with profound meaning and purpose and a sense of where we have come from that can assist us in responding to today's world with understanding and compassion.

For my contribution, I have aimed at an integration of several years of searching, studying and experience that draws on different fields and teachings about creativity. I briefly touch on Creation-Centred Spirituality that the radical theologian and Episcopal priest Matthew Fox has untiringly brought attention to over recent decades, along with other insights and wisdom I have found important because of a strong creative element to them that can assist in the healing process and a wholesome spiritual outlook, especially psychosynthesis psychology. Creativity can also be seen as profoundly interconnected to the green heart of all other chapters of this book.

In his chapter, Richard Adams gives a personal account of his many years as an experienced rambler. He mentions how walking in Nature frees up his bones. "Our bodies were meant to move" he pithily tells us. Initially inspired by Carl Jung's *Modern Man in Search of a Soul* and Joseph Cambell's *The Hero with a Thousand Faces*, Richard shares stories of times when he set forth on a journey equipped with Ordnance Survey maps, good walking boots, all-weather gear and a rucksack to explore places of natural and wild beauty. He shares experiences of some awesome times, such as when he embarked on the 100 mile long South Downs Way and 630 miles long South West Coast Path walks.

Piers Warren writes on one of the topics he is especially known for and informs us that the path of the gardener has become not just something he does but something he is. Importantly, Piers reminds us that gardening is an Earth-centred practice: "for without earth or soil there would be no plants and therefore no life or even atmosphere on this planet." He includes concerns he has about our planet's decline in biodiversity, the decrease in the number of wild creatures and plants, and how the reduction in populations of birds and insects are often highlighted yet things such as eco-sustainability and the use of harmful pesticides are not.

With lifelong experience of spiritual retreats, Chris Holmes informs us in his chapter how he has come to understand contemplation and action as being complementary. He recognises that the way of contemplation can lead to an inner and outer simplicity that puts us in touch with an intrinsic worth of both ourselves and all things, and how this is fundamental to a spiritually green way of living. He mentions the pitfalls as well as the benefits of an authentic contemplative life. For Chris, focusing attention on our more-than-human relations seems like a fundamental requirement for contemplative practices. For him, human life only makes sense if it is interwoven with countless ways of being alive with Earth's animals, plants and ecosystems that surround and are a part of us.

In the chapter on community, Hilary Norton reminds us that having a sense of belonging is vital for our psychological well-being, and can help us develop mature ways of being in our challenging world. Hilary writes about the variety of GreenSpirit activities such as conferences, retreats and seasonal celebrations, and how members can find inspiration, community and support, often in beautiful locations as well as online. She also shares information about the way GreenSpirit has changed over the years in response to global changes and individual and collective needs, and how GreenSpirit has been influenced by contemporary scientists and wisdom keepers such as Brian Swimme and Joanna Macy.

In the final chapter, Piers Warren and Ian Mowll share their views about green activism. Piers informs us that activism can take on many forms and offers down-to-earth steps that most people can do. Ian writes about what he sees as important, and how being the change he wants to see in the world is for him an essential part of his spiritual journey. He completes the chapter on an encouraging hopeful note by pointing out how "The world is changing rapidly and none of us can keep up with all of the changes. But by coming together and learning from each other, there is a chance that we can make the large-scale impacts which are so vital to the health of our planet and all living beings."

I trust that readers will find much food for spiritual inspiration, reflection and replenishment in the following pages. For details about other titles in the GreenSpirit Book Series, see the Resources section at the back of this book or visit the GreenSpirit Book Series webpage on GreenSpirit's website.

~ Santoshan (Stephen Wollaston)

* * *

1
The Way of Simplicity

Marian Van Eyk McCain

Simplicity, simplicity, simplicity! I say, let your affairs be as two or three, and not a hundred or a thousand; instead of a million count half a dozen, and keep your accounts on your thumb nail.
~ Henry David Thoreau

In character, in manner, in style, in all things, the supreme excellence is simplicity.
~ Henry Wadsworth Longfellow

Truth is ever to be found in simplicity, and not in the multiplicity and confusion of things.
~ Isaac Newton

Simplicity is the final achievement.
After one has played a vast quantity of notes and more notes, it is simplicity that emerges as the crowning reward of art.
~ Frederic Chopin

As psychologist Abraham Maslow pointed out, for us human beings the most basic need is for physical survival, and this will be the first thing that motivates our behaviour. For us, as for any other animal, the biological requirements for our survival are air, food, drink, shelter, sex, and sleep. And as a furless, warm-blooded species of animal, we humans also need clothing and warmth.

Maslow explained that beyond the basic needs for survival and safety, humans, as a social species, also have an emotional need for interpersonal relationships, affiliating, connectedness, and being part of a group. And as a highly intelligent and self-aware species, we have, unlike other animals, a need for feelings of self-worth, accomplishment, self-fulfilment, and personal, spiritual growth.

A baby's first action, milliseconds after birth, is to take a breath. Once breathing is established, the next action is to seek the nipple and, on finding it, suck milk – the primary, most basic and most simple food and yet one so full of nutrients that it alone can sustain that small body for the next few months. There may be many other people in that baby's life, but the only one who is indispensable at that point is the provider of milk.

As that child grows and matures, his or her diet gradually becomes more complex and so does every other aspect of his or her life – intellectual, emotional, interpersonal, social and so on. Yet how many of us, especially in young adulthood, are consciously aware of this gradual process of complexification? I certainly wasn't.

Not only has my own life become more complex as I aged, but life in general, particularly in our Western society has complexified more in my lifetime than ever before in history.

When I was born, plastic had not yet been invented. Neither had ballpoint pens. Even when I was in high school there was no TV or Internet. There were no mobile phones, no iPods, no jumbo jets, no microwave ovens. We did our laundry by hand or swished it around in a 'dolly tub,' put it through a wringer and hung it to dry on the washing line.

For a long time after I reached adulthood, I was unaware of the process of complexification that was going on all around me. I just went along with it like everybody else, enjoying all its advantages and not paying much attention to the effect it was starting to have on the planet. I didn't become aware of that aspect of it until I was in my thirties. As I wrote in *The Rising Water Project*:[1]

> *It was through wheeling my children to the shops in their battered old pram that my wake-up call came. Fruit flies had been (allegedly) spotted in the area and our local Council started spraying poison around the streets, right at the level of young bodies in prams. I was incensed. So were my neighbours. We got together, protested and got the spraying stopped. I read Rachel Carson's 'Silent Spring'. That, for me, was the turning point. That was when I first became conscious of the impact humans were having on our planet.*
>
> *By 1971, more 'green' books had started appearing and*

> *I devoured them eagerly. Friends of the Earth published their Environmental Handbook that year (I still have my ancient, yellowed copy). I went on to read 'Diet for a Small Planet' and then, the following year, 'Only One Earth', 'The Limits to Growth', and 'Blueprint for Survival', followed in 1973 by 'Small is Beautiful'. I was reborn as a greenie with the beginnings of conscious, global awareness.*

Since then, I have not only been active in the green movement but I have tried to live as simply and lightly on the Earth as I can – not just for environmental reasons but also because the more I opted for simplicity in all aspects of my life, the more full, rich and enjoyable my life became.

I should point out that 'simplicity' is not a simple concept. As I wrote in *The Lilypad List*,[2]

> *...if, for example, you ask people to describe what would be the most simple, basic, no-frills holiday they can think of, they will probably say a camping trip. Yet if you have ever planned and organised a camping trip you will know that a package tour to Spain – or even Africa – is really a much simpler option – at least for you, if not for the folks who set it up for you.*
>
> *So 'The Simple Life,' as most people imagine it, is not necessarily less trouble to live, or less trouble to organise. In fact it will probably take more planning, more thinking about and quite a lot more effort to live than the average, mainstream sort of lifestyle that most people have, in the same way that choosing dinner from the 'a la carte' menu*

> *takes more energy and forethought than saying 'I'll have the set meal, please.'*
>
> *There is really no difference between the package tour and the camping trip, because in each case someone has to organise it all. It is just that with the package tour, that part is hidden. From your point of view, it is a question of pay your money, collect your vouchers, tie on your luggage labels and go.*

So if we seek that other kind of simplicity – the simplicity of the camping trip, the home made bread and home grown vegetables from the garden – we have to take most of that complexity back on to ourselves.

Simplicity, for me, does not require that I turn my back on all the modern inventions that make our lives easier than they would have been a century ago. I love it that I can now send an email or a text message to someone I care about and get a response within hours or minutes, rather than having to write a letter, post it and wait days or even weeks. I love it that I can find out anything about anything by pressing a few keys on my computer instead of having to go to a library and scour the reference section. Simplicity, in the sense that I am employing that word here, is about placing one's emphasis on the quality of objects and experiences rather than on quantity. It is about mindfulness – being fully present for whatever we are doing/experiencing, moment to moment – and it is about delight.

Take food, for example. Of all the meals I have eaten in my life, there are two that particularly stand out. The first was when I was nine years old. Although WW2 was not completely over, our home town (Plymouth) was no longer being bombed, so my grandparents booked themselves a week's holiday in a farm near Looe, on the Cornish coast. After school on the Friday, my mother took me down to join them there. That evening, as I was getting ready for bed, the farmer's wife brought me a bedtime snack. It was the crust from a newly-baked loaf of bread, slathered in home-made butter, and a glass of milk that was still warm from the cow. That's all. I had never tasted anything more heavenly and I remember it vividly to this day. The second was a picnic lunch taken in 1977 on a hillside near Delphi, in Greece, and that, too, was the simplest meal imaginable: local bread, local goat's butter, local honey and fresh figs, washed down with fresh spring water. These memories illustrate what I have called – for want of a better name – the principle of delight.

The particular kind of delight that I am speaking of is more than just the ordinary delight you feel when something nice comes in the mail. It seems to have more dimensions than that. It is a feeling of fullness and aliveness and ordinary sacredness. Yes, it comes with the smell of baking bread, but it is more than just the delicious smell of baking bread. It is what you get when you combine the smell of the bread with the nutritional value of the wholewheat grains, the shape of the farmhouse loaf, the simplicity and solidity of an old-fashioned bread oven, the cosiness of the kitchen, the meditative movement of hands kneading dough and the love that goes into the baking. Add them all up, and the result is a sense of organic naturalness and simplicity and wholeness, which the word 'delight' cannot fully describe. But it will have to do, for now, since I can find no better one in our language. It is very similar to what the Japanese call *wabi-sabi* – the principle underlying those things of simple elegance for which the Japanese culture is so famous, such as ikebana (flower arrangement) and the tea ceremony; things of refinement which have yet retained their essential naturalness, their clear lines and rustic character.

A prerequisite for this kind of delight to arise in our lives is quiet attention to the moment, for the *wabi-sabi* quality can only be fully appreciated by a mind which is at once peaceful and yet fully attentive. When the bread is baked, we cannot savour it unless we rest into the process. To gobble it and rush on to the next activity is to miss the point – and miss out on the delight.

Twenty-two years after that Delphi picnic, visiting Greece again, I searched in vain for the goat's butter and the honey. The wonders of modern marketing had brought in butter from New Zealand and replaced the local honey with a large assortment of little plastic containers of Kraft spreads. I guess they call it progress, but to me it feels more like theft; the theft of delight. It made me sad; not only because the quality was lost, but because I know that the kind of food from which that humble picnic on the hillside was made is slowly being replaced, worldwide, by something less nutritious and less beautiful, for food can be beautiful, not only in its taste, but in the way it looks, the way it smells, the way it feels. And another experience, similar to the Delphi picnic, brought that home to me, right in the middle of a very ordinary day.

I belonged to an organic fruit and vegetable co op. It was at the unfashionable end of a dusty city street. A simple, unglamorous shop, with a cement floor and big wooden benches lined with boxes of produce. Most of the staff were volunteers who worked in return for generous discounts. It felt good in there. Customers chatted and smiled, weighing out their own produce and jotting down the prices themselves on little pads of scratch paper with stubby pencils attached. There were a few recycled bags. Many people, like me, brought baskets.

This particular morning, I had walked out of the co op with a full basket and was attaching it to the pack rack of my bicycle, when suddenly the sheer beauty of that basketful of fruit and vegetables made me stop and stare. It was like a piece of art. The dark green of the chard leaves and the bright yellow of the tiny squash that nestled among them, the earthy promise of the mushrooms, the translucent glow of the apples and carrots, all mixed together in the basket, suddenly took on an aura of beauty that surpassed any painting I had ever seen. Gifts of the field. How utterly beautiful they all looked, sitting there together, a colourful cornucopia of nourishment. Remembering other places I had lived, other ways I had shopped, remembering Styrofoam and shrink-wrap, plastic bags inside plastic bags, I felt suddenly overwhelmed by emotion. It was as though blessings were raining down upon my head. A golden, glowing moment of delight.

I realized in that moment, standing beside my bicycle, that living lightly and simply is not just about being kinder to the Earth and obediently doing the right thing, ecologically. It is about pure pleasure. It is about stopping and noticing and being aware, for it is through that very awareness that the delight begins to flow. It came to me, right then, as I stood there smiling at my fruit and vegetables, that for me to have to buy them at the supermarket would actually be to deprive myself of something wonderful.

I love those special moments. When I have dozed off into mindlessness, they wake me up again, like alarm clocks, bringing new messages of wisdom. They recall me to aliveness, inviting me into wonderment and into the fullness of living. And they can happen any time. Even in the middle of the shopping.

Just as hastily gobbling that fresh bread rules out the delight of savouring it, mindful, delight-filled experiences often require slowing down. And never more so than with travel. Paradoxically, although you might think that the 'simplest' way to cover a long distance is to fly, travelling that way tends to rule out the kind of simple delight that I have been describing. For that, we need to travel more slowly, the same way I travelled on my first visit to Italy way back in 1958, nearly 40 years before the establishment of easyJet or Eurostar.

Italy, for me, is the land I finally reached when I had stood on a ferry deck watching Dover's white cliffs slowly fade, traversed, on a steam train, a large section of France, and passed through those luscious Swiss valleys with their emerald grass, chocolate-box villages and the sound of cowbells in clear air. Italy is what lay before me when our train finally came down through the Alps on to the plain of Lombardy. Even though nowadays, thanks to Eurostar, the journey is a little shorter, Italy, for me, is still a far place lying a day, a night and most of another day from home. The blue jewel they call the Mediterranean is a reward it takes many hours and many turns of the wheels to earn.

Travelling that way gives our body clocks time to adjust. It gives us a true sense of distance and the size of the world, as did my five-week ocean voyage from Southampton to Melbourne in the same year that I first went to Italy. Mainly, though, instead of flying above everything at forty thousand feet it gives us the opportunity to soak in and to savour the changing scenery and to record those glimpses of beautiful mountainsides, tumbling waterfalls, serene lakes, city streets, beaches and seascapes that will live in our memories like photos in an album.

These same principles of slowing down and mindfulness – and the savouring of experiences that so often result from employing them – can also be applied to many other aspects of our lives, such as shelter (I once wrote a poem about the simplicity of the cottage I live in), belongings (why fill our house with consumer goods and then have to 'declutter'?), exercise (taking walks outdoors and attending to the sights and sounds around us instead of using a treadmill at the gym), socializing (a quiet dinner with special friends rather than a wild party) – and so on.

In fact all those needs that Maslow listed can be fulfilled

by these principles. And I have a feeling that if we were to make that our mission we might find that as well as greatly enriching our own lives we would also be doing what is best for our beautiful Earth. For me, that clinches it. I shall go on living simply till I die. And I hope my dying will be simple too.

* * *

1. Title number seven in the GreenSpirit Book Series, compiled by Ian Mowll.
2. Title number twelve in the GreenSpirit Book Series, by Marian McCain.

Editor's Note

For further reading about the Way of Simplicity, Marian's two books about her many years' experience of downshifting and the simple life, *The Lilypad List: 7 steps to the simple life* (GreenSpirit, 2021), and *Downshifting Made Easy: How to plan for your planet-friendly future* (Earth Books, 2011), are highly recommended.

2
The Way of Storytelling

Ian Mowll

We are the cosmos made conscious and life is the means by which the universe understands itself.
~ Professor Brian Cox

Way back in the mists of time, there was a traveller who set out on a journey. As he walked along, there, on the side of the path was a stone cutter. The traveller asked the worker, "What are you doing?"

The man was very discontented with his hard work, and he replied, "I'm cutting these huge stones with these tools and putting them together as I've been told to do. I'm sweating in this heat and my back is hurting. What's more, I'm bored, and I don't want to do this meaningless job".

The traveller continued on his journey, and he came across another stone cutter. He asked the same question, "What are you doing?"

The worker replied, "I have a wife and children, so every day I cut these boulders into regular shapes. It's repetitive but it helps to feed my family and that's all I want".

Again, the traveller continued on his journey until he came to yet another stone cutter on the side of the path. Again, he asked, "What are you doing?"

The third worker's eyes were blazing with excitement and his muscles were taught with his exacting work. He paused, he pointed up towards the sky and said, "I am building a cathedral!"

This simple story shows how we may be faced with similar tasks, yet it's the stories we tell ourselves that can either throw us into the depths of despair or lift us up to embrace life with enthusiasm, courage and compassion. Helpful stories, more than intellect, can fuel our instincts and emotions and give us the spiritual energy we may need to pursue our goals and transform restrictive perceptions.

History

It is probable that ever since modern humans developed language, we shared stories – maybe around a campfire at the end of the day. These stories would help orientate people on their journey through life and help bind a tribe together with familiar community-affirming stories that they all shared. So, it is not surprising that the great spiritual traditions have treasured and used certain stories to inspire their followers, such is the power of life-affirming storytelling.

Today, traditional storytelling has morphed into such

things as soap operas, fiction books and films. Modern spiritual traditions also use stories, and if these are told well, they can help us make sense of our world, feed our creative imagination and inspire us to build a better world.

Why Stories?

So why do we have stories? Why don't we just tell each other bald facts and dispense with all the embellishments of a story? I believe there are several reasons for this.

Have you noticed how your nighttime dreams are virtually always in a story format? They rarely take the shape of direct statements or commands. Maybe our nighttime stories are seeking to encourage us to reflect, to engage with our stories, and to explore and process the underlying meaning of our dreams' imagery and events. Maybe they have multiple interpretations – giving us more opportunities to respond creatively to the message of our dreams. Maybe they are making connections between our lives and different ways of looking at situations, helping us to piece together life's fragments into something more coherent and holistically whole.

For me, dreams help me to connect with the mystical realms beyond us. For some people (and I include myself in this), it sometimes feels as though a dream comes from some level of consciousness outside my daily experience of life. This enables me to feel supported on my journey, that I am part of a wider life force and part of my purpose in life is to be regenerated by this mystical energy.

And finally, maybe dreams 'speak' in metaphors because

the mystery of life is so deep, so profound, that the answer to some of life's questions cannot be explained simply by logic. We need the signposts of metaphor to point the way on our journeys through life. More than this, metaphors can expand our ways of being by opening us up to new possibilities, which is crucial as we require creative responses to the many challenges of today's world.

Why Do We Need Stories?

The world is complex and sometimes a simple story can help a large group of people – who may not even know each other – to act with a common purpose. One example is that we have a shared story that England exists. England is a human construct; as astronauts often comment when they look down at the Earth, there is no physical line drawn between countries, we have created these 'lines' in our imagination. But the story that England exists means, for instance, that people in England know that there is a government responsible for the country, that they can travel within its borders with set laws and customs and that they need passports to travel abroad. This shared story provides a level of coherent activity even with complete strangers.

Stories don't just help us with practicalities. Storytelling when done well inspires us to respond to an ever-changing world in a meaningful way. Whilst the written word can help to disseminate ideas, but when they are endlessly repeated, they can become stuck. It can also be said that some parts of mainstream spiritual traditions have become stuck with their written words, words that were written thousands of years ago when the times and societal challenges were very different to today. Storytelling, however, can change and adapt to new circumstances in the world. David Abram writes about this in his book The Spell of the Sensuous and he says that, by implication, we need less written words and more storytelling in our spirituality so that it is fresh and relevant to today's world, as well as creative enough to adapt as new contemporary knowledge and wisdom surfaces.

Personal Spiritual Journey

I sometimes perform as a storyteller. And I agree with what some other storytellers say that it can feel as though stories come through me as the storyteller rather than me simply narrating a series of events. When I am performing at my best, I feel like a conduit for a story that lives in the mystical realms beyond us. It feels as though images, feelings and instincts flow through me, and I have a deep sense of relaxation and connection. It's no longer about my ego but about my connection with that which is beyond. It's a wonderful, life-affirming feeling, as through awakening to that connection I feel part of the greater life force of the Universe.

The Universe Story – a Story for Our Time

Stories underpin spiritual traditions and, as the world changes, we need stories that resonate with today's world and give us a sense of meaning and purpose. The world has changed a great deal in modern times; examples include the discovery of stars and galaxies, the Big Bang and the evolution of life on Earth. The Universe Story – the story as revealed by science from the Big Bang through to today could be seen as a modern creation story, giving us a sense of where we have come from and how we can respond to today's world with understanding and compassion.

There is much that can be said about this story – if you want a comprehensive overview, read the small but excellent book in the low-cost GreenSpirit Book Series: *The Universe Story in Science and Myth* by Greg Morter and Niamh Brennan.[1] Here are just a couple of aspects of this story to highlight its relevance to today's world:

- The Universe Story opens me up to awe and wonder. The long timeframe (13.8 billion years), the vast size of the Universe, the intricate weaving together of atoms and molecules to form early life and then the wonderous evolutionary leaps that propelled life to its current manifestation, amazes me and opens my heart to all of creation. This inspires me to want to take care of our planet Earth and all life, to protect it and, as best I can, leave it in a good state for future generations.

- The Universe Story also informs me how all life evolved from one single common ancestor, a cell of life that appeared around 4 billion years ago. This highlights that I am related to all life on Earth and because of this interconnection I feel morally and ethically deeply moved to do what I can to protect the natural world and her abundant and awesome biodiversity. More than this, I recognize that we humans are all one tribe. This is not just a fascinating fact, but can inspire all of us to move away from nationalism and to see ourselves as 'citizens of planet Earth'. And because of this, it follows that we need to face the current ecological crisis, including climate change, 'together' as one species as no one country can implement the changes that are needed to combat climate change alone.

Practical Action

So, how can stories make real changes for a better world? About 25 years ago, when I understood the urgent need for action on climate change and other environmental challenges such as species loss, I thought that telling people the bald facts would change many of their minds. I was wrong! Whilst facts are an essential underpinning of any viewpoint, generally, they don't tend to inspire. They often don't stir the deep waters of the soul to change someone's outlook.

I have found two effective ways of bringing about changes in people's understanding. Firstly, by personal example. We humans are highly social animals, in fact we depend on each other for our survival. So, we take notice of what others do – particularly people we know. Showing that I am personally concerned about the world by what I do can be one of the most effective ways of influencing others.

Secondly, by telling stories. I sometimes do eco-storytelling to try to inspire others to act on environmental issues. One of these is the story of King Canute. He was a King of England who tried to stop the incoming tide simply by shouting at the waves and commanding them to stop. Of course, this did not work; the tide came in regardless of his protestations. The King used this to show that, contrary to his courtiers' praise of him, he was only human and nothing greater. Not only does this story show us that we do not have power over the natural world, but it implies that we need to work with Nature and the Earth for the benefit of all life. For me, this story also has a mythological aspect, as rising water in dreams can be about instincts and emotions claiming their rightful place in our psyche. Our western world is sometimes too dominated by rational thinking and I personally see a need for us humans to feel connected to the underlying instincts and creative forces of Nature so that we are again, like our distant ancestors, 'one with the Earth'.

Conclusion

Stories are like rivers, sustaining life and ever-changing. We need to embrace and flow with them to give us the emotional capacity to face the challenges of today's global ecological problems. I'll end with a quote which, I hope, sums up my chapter for this book:

> *The stories we tell literally make the world. If you want to change the world, you need to change your story. This truth applies both to individuals and institutions.*
>
> ~ Michael Margolis

* * *

1. Title number three in the GreenSpirit Book Series.

Further Reading

Stina Gray, *When the Woods Sang: Returning to the Singing Earth*, Campano Edizioni, 2023.

3
The Way of Creativity

Santoshan aka Stephen Wollaston

Life is short, and we have but a brief time in which to explore, to learn, to experience, and to create. Let us make the most of that time, and let us burn brightly, like meteors across the night sky, leaving behind us a trail of light and inspiration for those who come after us.
~ Jack London

...the creative impulse is not restricted to people who are active in the arts. Creativity describes an approach to the whole of life, allowing playfulness and spontaneity to enter our lives; accepting some slack; letting go of the need to control and direct every move. Creativity is living adventurously.
~ Jennifer Kavanagh

One of my earliest memories is a nightmare I had when I was six years old of a devil-like caricature figure destructively driving a bulldozer through a hilly green countryside. The figure had one of those grins that baddies in films often have as he aggressively churned-up a place of natural beauty and turned it into a barren landscape. At such a young age, I didn't know what to make of it, yet its vivid visual impact surprisingly stayed with me over the years. As an adult, I recognised its prophetic message about the way greed and a lack of compassion, care and concern for the natural world were becoming greater evils in human history and how they needed to be addressed. My motivation behind the creative work I do as a writer, editor and typographer for GreenSpirit and to co-help in other ways as an active member of its community, is in seeing the work as a form of sacred activism with a focus on promoting Earth-centred awareness. Green spirituality for me is both a cause and a path of wisdom I feel passionate about and consider crucial for our times.

Something else happened in my early school years. I began to feel a need to be alone in my bedroom and be still and quiet and focus my attention on pencil drawing or being creative in different ways such as building miniature houses, bridges and other structures with colourful toy bricks and Lego. What I didn't realise at the time is that I had quite naturally discovered 'art as meditation', as well as creativity's links with play and revealing solutions, and using creativity as a way of exploring and expressing deeper parts of myself. I also felt a sense of awe and wonder when contemplating various activities of Nature in my parents' council house garden. I would later come to understand how creativity is interwoven with spiritual living and wellbeing, and the profound sacredness of Nature. Regarding play, I've noticed it can appear a bit like indecisiveness at first (a period of not knowing) when used to explore possibilities but in fact allows for an organic emerging of fresh perspectives and creative outcomes.

Expressions of Creativity

For us humans, dreams, poetry, music and visual and physical arts, such as dance, are things that speak to us in ways that language cannot, and can bring us together in common causes for good – as the influence of my dream/ prophetic nightmare partly did. It is one of the reasons why they are valued in GreenSpirit.

When I began exploring various spiritual and mystical paths and practices of the East and West in my late teens, I soon realised they held important teachings about transforming and transcending restrictive patterns of being that feed unhealthy egocentric behaviour such as greed and a lack of compassion.

Such teachings often highlight a oneness with life, including the natural world, and the responsibilities we share for all sentient beings and preserving Nature's biodiversity and essential ecosystems. In India for example, numerous species, trees, forests, rivers and mountains have long-been considered as especially holy and important to protect. In Hindu Yoga philosophy, *Shakti* is seen as a creative divine mother energy that is continuously active in the Universe and Nature. As a Christian, the 20th century French priest, mystic and palaeontologist Pierre Teilhard de

Chardin saw Christ as the creative energy and loving heart of the Cosmos, with the power to unite all people, life and things together and animate them into new expressions of community.

Eastern and Western psychology and spiritual views about Nature, our individuality, and cosmological creativity also led me to study psychosynthesis psychology (whose founder, Roberto Assagioli, held strong eco-centred beliefs and a panentheistic understanding of divinity) and train as a psychosynthesis counsellor, as I found the school comparable to Yogic teachings, including Sri Aurobindo's Integral Yoga and the insights of various mystics I've been drawn to. Through my training and counselling work, I've seen more people coming to therapy suffering from eco-anxiety, and witnessed, as other psychosynthesis practitioners have also noticed, how creativity profoundly influences healing, and seen how therapy itself is a creative process, of which psychosynthesis psychology offers various activities that enhances it.[1]

The American academic and novelist Theodore Roszak is often credited as being the first to use the term 'ecopsychology', which has its roots in early 20th century schools of psychology and become more prominent in recent decades. In Roszak's book *The Voice of the Earth* he highlights how consciously awakening to deep interconnections with Nature improves psychological wellbeing. He also looks at destructive environmental human behaviour and its underlying causes.

Creation Spirituality

There are sound reasons why the creative energies of dreams, art and Nature have been drawn upon since ancient times, as early cave paintings and indigenous cultures' appreciation and cherishing of dreams, art and the natural world show a special awareness of. In recent times psychologists such as Carl Jung have highlighted the benefits of working with archetypes, dreams and free-drawing, and the term 'wild imagination' has come into use to describe positive aspects of creative processes.[2]

The cultural ecologist and geophilosopher David Abram and late conservationist and founder member of Schumacher College Stephan Harding came together with others in their work for the Alliance for Wild Ethics. Motivated by a love of Nature, they sought to ease the spread of human destruction of Earth by employing the arts and natural sciences to deeply influence shifts in human behaviour and consciousness. Yet I do not wish to give the impression that creativity is solely about imagination, dreams and art, as creativity is in everything that we do and an essential part of all life. For us humans, it connects strongly with internal reflections, feelings, intuitions and processes that lead to bringing something new into being, including not only artistic objects but healthy changes in our thinking, feelings, actions and behaviour, including our interrelationship with Earth.

The radical theologian and Episcopal priest Matthew Fox wrote about the psychologist Carl Rogers in his book *Creativity* and how Rogers's experience of working as a therapist placed him in tune with forces of the Universe and elicited a feeling of awe within him, which Rogers saw as interconnected with an emergence of the self. This fits with my own understanding of creativity as being written into the Universe, into all of Earth-life, ways of being and daily activities and interactions, which can be read into Rogers's experience and connected with creative flow and expression, which happens when we are fully present and let go of fears and inhibitions.

Fox, as some GreenSpirit members will be aware, started to look into and clarify a four-fold path of mysticism in the 60s and 70s (his college mentor Père Chenu suggested the term 'Creation-Centred Spirituality' to describe it), which drew on teachings of early Christian Nature mystics such as Hildegard of Bingen and Francis of Assisi, as well as mystics and teachings from other traditions of both the East and West, including contemporary science and psychology, and Earth-centred wisdom of indigenous cultures.

Fox, like other green focused teachers, has highlighted how we do not in fact *live on Earth* but are *a part of Earth*, and when we create in wholesome ways, we take part in, celebrate and create with the creative forces of the Universe and Nature that have their origins in the initial bursting forth of the Big Bang.

Along with others, I found the teachings and progressive inclusiveness Fox highlighted inspiring. His wisdom resonated with me at a time when I needed it in a search for a contemporary spirituality relevant for our time.

It motivated me to find an organisation in the UK that embraced the ideas of Creation-Centred Spirituality and is what led me to GreenSpirit.

Four Interlinked Pathways

Since the release of Fox's groundbreaking book *Original Blessing* in '83, he has tirelessly clarified and promoted the interactive fourfold path of Creation Spirituality, which can be summarised as:

1. The *via positiva*, the way of awe, delight and amazement.
2. The *via negativa*, the way of uncertainty, darkness, suffering and letting go.
3. The *via creativa*, the way of birthing, creativity and passion.
4. The *via transformativa*, the way of justice, healing and celebration.

Number three, the *via creativa*, is obviously significant to the topic of this chapter, and from where Creation Spirituality gets its name. The below passage by Fox highlights his mystical and cosmological understanding of creativity:

> *When one moves from introspective psychology to a cosmic one and from a state of an emerging one and from a repression of human creativity to a welcoming of the divine power of creativity in humans, one unleashes much that is hidden. Much that is charged and exciting… The powers*

> *we humans have to give birth to our images are in fact the very divine power of the universe itself and, more than that, of the divinity itself.*

In the early parts of the last century, common sources of creative expression were often looked upon as unhealthy drives, urges, desires and emotions emerging from lower levels of our unconscious. In contrast, the founder of psychosynthesis, Assagioli, recognised, as Fox does, that creativity originating from our *higher consciousness* does not arise in the same way and has more meaningful and life-enhancing potential that assists in bringing new and healthy ways of being into existence. Assagioli pointed out two ways in which this can occur: *a descent* of the higher Self to our personal 'I', or *an ascent* of our individual 'I'-self to the higher Self – both of which activate creativity that can achieve a healthy wholeness.

Psychosynthesis psychologist James Vargiu described creativity as a *core process* that is seen *in the process* rather than objects. In addition, Carl Rogers emphasised the importance of flexibility and being open to experience for a condition of *constructive* creativity that fosters potential. For creativity can be either healthy and healing, or unhealthy and dangerous if used in ways to be more destructive and manipulative and harm others for self-gain, or bring beneficial changes into being and give birth to what is joyful and enriching. The Universe also exhibits forces of creativity and destruction, and Earth has its cycles of new life, death and regrowth.

Cultivating Creativity

Although we can be drawn into stories that justify harmful and restrictive patterns that keep us stuck in unwholesome ways of being, higher forms of creativity do not flow from inhibiting patterns but emerge in new ways and actions that grow from our unique individuality, as well as from individual groups and movements and unique events and circumstances. For in addition to taking place on an individual level, it can be seen happening collectively in times of great social change such as the recognition of gay, racial and women's rights in the West, and also with people coming together for environmental reasons.

A healthy approach involves interacting with numerous areas of growth that enlarge who we are and lead us to previously unrecognised potential to discover new realms of possibility and transformation, and move beyond restrictive patterns and realise that change and growth are always possible. In many ways it's about knowing ourselves – physically, mentally and emotionally – as the inscription above the entrance to the Oracle at the Temple of Apollo in Delphi wisely reminded visitors, which is a crucial piece of sound advice for those of us who are consciously seeking greater awareness on spiritual paths.

Five Stages

In writing on creativity, Vargiu expanded a previous four-stage model by adding the fifth stage to the following list:

1. Preparation
2. Frustration
3. Incubation
4. Illumination
5. Elaboration

Preparation is an initial stage of conscious work that *attempts* to put things into order and arrive at a solution but *cannot*. This leads to a blocked stage of frustration related to the inability to change things and have awareness of another way of being and/or approach. Of interest is what Vargiu highlights about an awareness of the 'creative field' that is present in all stages – implying the potential for both healing and wholesome creativity is always there and available – which he links with Nature's evolution and mystics' descriptions of a Universal Mind that assists in the unfoldment of new ideas and patterns, and helps to foster creativity and new life. Yet this is not about *forcing something to happen* but being *open to conducive conditions* that assist in creative unfoldment.

After frustration comes an incubation stage. On the surface it may appear little is happening, like seeds in the soil needing time to germinate before sprouting. Artists often experience this, as I have myself, by doing something else such as sleeping or going for a walk in a park or the countryside to take one's mind off finding a solution, which allows time for our unconscious to influence a creative outcome. Since the Covid pandemic, more people have come to discover the various benefits of Nature.

Illumination happens in chance intuitions that suggest a previously unforeseen way forward. It often appears as if coming from outside ourselves, which also occurs in peak and mystical experiences. Drawing on an analogy of magnetic fields to demonstrate what can happen with the influence of the creative field, Vargiu points out how the appearance of two opposing parts will come together in an organised meaningful pattern, bringing harmony, simplicity and beauty – formed by the field's influential creative energy, which plays a key role in creative processes, including creative flow.

In the final stage, elaboration activates what has newly surfaced and helps us to be more grounded, holistic in mind, body and feelings, and integrate a healthier outlook and creative life. Of importance is how Vargiu sees imagination, which is also influential in dreams and various creative activities, as a bridge between our mind and feelings, which can release blocked stages of creativity and influence a new way of being, meaning and purpose to life – a way of dialoguing with our higher Self that assists in therapeutic and spiritual transformation.

Using Our Creativity for a Greater Good

We now stand in a position where we are called to be involved in the making of a New Earth Community, which the geologian Thomas Berry often promoted and termed 'the Great Work'.[3] Our current times require us to embrace an inclusive, universal and creative spirituality: one that encompasses living our lives as skilfully, wisely and compassionately as possible, and involves recognising the profound interrelationship we share with all people and Nature and the responsibilities this brings.

The wisdom of various Nature-centred traditions such as GreenSpirit often highlights transforming, compassionate and universal aspects of spirituality that have always been there inviting us to awaken to their life-enriching possibilities; they are expressions of Supreme Creativity that can be manifested in every area and day of our life. It is a creativity that embraces an array of activities and types of unfoldment without undermining an understanding of an essential oneness to life, and involves a multitude of disciplines and practices that will overlap and interlink for many people, such as mystical, therapeutic, scientific and artistic areas of growth.

Closing Reflection

If we consider how the Universe came into being and how it is holistic, integral and forever in the process of evolving, we come to realise how it is an important part of who we are, as we are all incredible products of the Universe and its awe-inspiring creativity. We in fact already possess all that we need to be in a healthy interactive relationship with the creativity of all life. Although it can require deep psychological and therapeutic work to arrive at, we only need to unfold the intuitive insight, understanding and awareness that is called for to overcome the appearance of separation from it. The creative impulse within us will take on greater meaning when our actions are performed as expressions of spiritual living and a recognition of our interconnected unity with all – with human and more-than-human life.

* * *

1. Paper on creative exercises used by Catherine Ann Lombard and Barbara CN Müller, *Opening the Door to Creativity: A Psychosynthesis Approach*. Available at lombard-mc3bcller-psychosynthesis-and-creativity-accepted-by-jhp.pdf, 2016 (downloaded 30th January 2023).

2. Psychotherapist Allan Frater has begun teaching about wild imagination. His book *Waking Dreams: Imagination in Psychotherapy and Everyday Life* touches on related areas though does not use the term itself. Published by TransPersonal Press, 2021.

3. Geologian is a term Thomas Berry used to describe himself. See *The Great Work: Our Way into the Future* for his central teachings. Published by Bell Tower, 1999.

References

Roberto Assagioli, *Psychosynthesis: A Manual of Principals and Techniques*. Aquarian Press, San Fransico, 1993.

Matthew Fox, *Creativity: Where the Divine and the Human Meet.* Tarcher/Penguin, 2002.

Matthew Fox, *Original Blessing: A Primer in Creation Spirituality.* Tarcher/Putnam, 2002.

Carl Rogers, *On Becoming a Person: A Therapists View of Psychotherapy.* Houghton Mifflin Company, 1961.

Theodore Roszak, *The Voice of the Earth: An Exploration of Ecopsychology*. Touchstone, 1993.

James Vargiu, *Creativity*, Synthesis Journal 3-4: *The Realization of the Self.* California Press, 1977.

Further Reading

David Abram, *The Spell of the Sensuous*, Vintage Books, 1997.

Sri Aurobindo (edited by AS Dalal/foreword by Ken Wilber), *A Greater Psychology: An Introduction to the Psychological Thought of Sri Aurobindo.* Tarcher/Putnam, 2001.

Stephan Harding, *Gaia Alchemy: The Reuniting of Science, Psyche, and Soul*, Bear & Company, 2022.

Curtis D Smith, *Jung's Quest for Wholeness: A Religious and Historical Perspective.* New York Press, 1990.

Pierre Teilhard de Chardin, *Pierre Teilhard de Chardin: Writings Selected with an Introduction by Ursula King.* Orbis Books, 1999.

4
The Way of Rambling

Richard Adams

It's your road and yours alone.
Others may walk it with you,
but no one can walk it for you.
~ Rumi

Stepping Forth

I grew up in the heart of London. I knew little of the country I lived in especially the wilder places. One Easter holiday my secondary school took me on a two-week trip that introduced me to long distance walks. The Ridgeway is an ancient trackway, the M1 of its day, used by traders and travellers for some five thousand years. It runs for 87 miles following a ridge of chalk hills from Overton Hill, Wiltshire, to Ivinghoe Beacon, northwest of London. But it adjoins other tracks that can take you further to the West and Wales to the North, and to the South and East coasts. It passes many Neolithic, Iron and Bronze Age sites including tombs and the giant 400-foot White Horse carved out of a chalk hillside near Uffington. The start, at the stone circles of Avebury, is a dramatic one. It certainly sparked my curiosity; why would people bring such a thing into being? To stand with a standing stone felt like I was starting a conversation across the millennia with someone who left this land mark so that they might reach out to me in the now. I felt close to our ancestors, sharing an alignment with them all the way up to the ageless stars. A connection was forged with the land and the peoples of the land that felt new and tangible to me – not something I dared mention to my fellow school mates. Looking back, it seemed like a sense of the sacred had surfaced in me. I felt a calling away from the suffocating secular city to the inspirational great outdoors.

The Initiation

There is something about a long walk which frees up my bones. Our bodies were meant to move. This primal activity is deeply ingrained. On a long walk my body seems to find its own pace and rhythm grounding and connecting me with the Earth. I have time to wander and not have to worry about being somewhere at some time. My chattering mind subsides, and my walking starts to walk me like a moving mantra. Now there is space to wander and enjoy the journey. On the Ridgeway I discovered how to step into the therapeutic. It took a little while to shift into this receptive state, about three days before Nature seemed to begin revealing herself to me, beetle by beetle, butterfly by butterfly, flower by flower. I found that I could gather something from this awareness that would be there to call on after I returned to the city. An initiation had started. I was becoming one of Nature's pilgrims.

The following Summer, my appetite wonderfully whetted, I walked the South Downs way where I encountered the land meeting the sea in an expansive spectacular way. The 100 mile long South Downs Way follows old routes and droveways along the chalk ridge north of the Sussex and Hampshire seaside towns. The way extends from Eastbourne to Winchester. I caught a train to Eastbourne and planned to overnight at Youth Hostels. There were more Hostels along the way back then. Walking around eight to ten miles per day took me about twelve days. The weather was fine, and sunshine warmed my striding pretty much throughout.

The breathtaking exhilaration of the brilliant white chalk cliffs of Beachy Head, 531 feet above the drumming waves of the English Channel, lives in me still. Its name is a French corruption of *beau chef* or 'beautiful headland' and full of beauty it is. To the west rolls more steep undulating cliffs known as the Seven Sisters. In fact, there are more than seven, but you don't always want to think about how many ups and downs when you are walking them!

I had learnt how to map read and use an orienteering baseplate compass. Sat Nav for walkers was a technical leap away. Equipped with my paper Ordnance Survey 1:25000 outdoor leisure maps, boots, and all-weather gear tucked into my frame supported rucksack, I felt ready to brave any pain, danger or unpleasant conditions that might come my way. Maps are interesting don't you think? They help us to orient ourselves. They help us find our position in relation to unfamiliar places. Maps are a way of finding out where we are and where we want to be – profoundly useful really. They also help us to find our path through new surroundings, tracing our adventure, and enabling us to find our way back home.

Around this time, the mid-1970's, my reading was articulating my inner journeying. I was introduced to the work of Carl Gustav Jung, particularly *Modern Man in Search of a Soul* and Joseph Cambell's *The Hero with a Thousand Faces*. It seemed my marching and meaning making were in step. Jung defined the psyche as the totality of psychic processes, conscious as well as unconscious. He went on to describe psychic patterns or archetypes present in our psyche. One such archetype is the Pilgrim who is the seeker, the iconoclast, the one who aims to find their authentic self by exploring the world. I was not conscious of it at the time, but I was acting out Cambell's Hero's Journey. Such stories are our journey through time and space to integrate who we are. The adventure model that we see in many mythological stories has stages. Firstly, a stepping forth from separateness to an encounter with the sacred, a life/death testing initiation, and then the return home renewed, transformed and complete, often with a gift to offer others.

The gift I received from the South Downs was the elemental experience of expansiveness. On this walk the sea is usually in sight. Here I was up on high with a 360-degree vision of the edge of the English Channel married to the sunlit verdant, rolling, land. No difficulty finding my way here. It was as simple as the water to my left and the land to my right, with the white chalk path revealed by the feet of those who have gone before. I knew then that being in Nature and walking the coastline of the island where I lived was something I needed to do. I would walk the peripheral edge in order to find my centre.

The following year I said goodbye to Hampshire and walked the Dorset coast path. This path had evolved as a route for coastguards patrolling for smugglers. As a result, it hugs the coastline providing excellent views of coves, inlets and caves. Since 1978 it has become part of the 630 miles long South West Coast Path National Trail. For my part, I simply acquired Ordnance Survey maps and followed the green dotty lines by the sea.

I started at Bournemouth from which I got the Sandbanks ferry to Studland Bay. Now toting the smallest tent and lightest camping stove I could find. I was ready to wild camp when needed. Nine days and some ninety miles later I reached the Golden Cap. It is arguably the highest point on the south coast of England at 627 feet. I arrived late in the day and needed to camp before sunset. I found a sheltered inconspicuous spot, made some soup, and watched the awesome sun go down in the kaleidoscopic sky.

The Gift

During the night I heard some rustling close to my head from outside of the tent. Not quite awake I stuck my head out to meet with another head! We both recoiled, scratching and scurrying before looking out again and catching each other's eyes. Looking into the stillness there stood a deer motionless some twenty yards away looking over its shoulder back at me. Transfixed we gazed at each other. I felt an intense sense of recognition through this encounter as I became aware of the roe deer and the roe deer became aware of me, from which a sudden deep feeling of enchantment seemed to magically fill the air.

The moment expanded to a vivid awareness of the gorse, grass, heathland and sea mist that were all present in the experience and mutually revealing each other. The relaxed deer lowered her head and pulled at some foliage, chewing mouthful by mouthful as the dawn ripened as she drifted easily away. A wordless, mythopoetic, revelatory, eco-spiritual encounter had happened. Do you remember as children how we all, in our hearts, knew that the Earth was alive? I was grateful for the remembrance.

The Return Bearing Gifts

Over the years, I tried to fit in a couple of week-long distance walks each Easter and Summer. I completed the South West Coast Path. Next, I travelled the remote Wales Coast Path; the coast paths around the Lake District; Northumberland; Yorkshire; Lincolnshire; and East Anglia. In between I started to do day walks from the Thames down the estuary and around the Kent and Essex coastline. Along the way I got to know more and more medicinal herbs and was able to offer their healing properties to others. There are still some pockets, mostly urban and industrial, that I am unlikely to do. Nevertheless, over a period of fifty years I reckoned to have walked some two and a half thousand miles. Coming up to date and nicely on cue, the England Coast Path National Trail is near completion. It will be the longest managed coastal path in the world. About 2,700 miles long, it will go all the way around the coast of England. It aims to link iconic places and heritage and will unlock some parts of our coast for the first time.

For me the greatest recreation, resourcing and resilience-making experience is rambling in Nature. Here the deepest parts of me come to life. In such moments, the periphery and the centre are joined, and I am made whole. Rambling, I feel, is a spiritual journey into the heart space, that place of a loving attention that goes nowhere in particular but ends up relating to everywhere. It is ultimately a revelatory experience. In the words of the geologian and priest Thomas Berry:

> *We will recover our sense of wonder and our sense of the sacred only if we appreciate the universe beyond ourselves as a revelatory experience of that numinous presence whence all things come into being.*

* * *

Further Reading

Nick Mayhew-Smith and Guy Hayward, *Britain's Pilgrim Places: The first complete guide to every spiritual treasure*. Lifestyle Press, 2022.

Christopher Somerville, Coast: *A Celebration of Britain's Coastal Heritage*. BBC Books, 2005.

Jake Tyler, *A Walk from the Wild Edge*. Penguin, 2022.

5
The Way of Gardening

Piers Warren

Food is sacred. We need to be connected with soil…
~ Satish Kumar

Ever since I was given a tiny patch of soil in my parents' garden when I was little, I knew growing plants was something I would do for the rest of my life. Sowing lettuce and radish seeds and watching them germinate into something beautiful and good to eat seemed miraculous and that wonder has never left me.

Gardening is truly an Earth-centred practice – for without earth or soil there would be no plants and therefore no life or even atmosphere on this planet. As gardeners, whether we have a large plot, an allotment, a balcony or just a few houseplants we have both a responsibility and an opportunity to practise in a way that benefits the health of the planet. Scientific studies show that it can really work, for example the biodiversity of life on allotments is higher than the general countryside.

We've known for some time that intensive agriculture is behind the crashes in many wildlife species over the last hundred years or so, and the last few decades in particular. It pains me greatly that the largest declines in biodiversity and numbers of wild creatures and plants have happened during my lifetime. The reduction in populations of birds and insects are often highlighted but whole ecological food webs are collapsing as key components are removed by pesticides, loss of habitat, pollution and so on. The amount of land used by agriculture in the UK is usually calculated as somewhere between 60 and 70%, which is huge compared to the 5% used by residential gardens. But not only can that 5% provide safe haven for many threatened species, but by learning to grow in an Earth-centred way we gardeners can help educate and influence others to act in a more environmentally friendly way.

Having said that there are many pitfalls facing gardeners today, for example, plants bought from a garden centre may have been grown in other countries, treated with various chemicals and have a high carbon footprint before they even reach your garden. For many years now it has been important to me to garden in a way that is kind to all life, even if it means sharing some of my plants and produce with other creatures. In fact it is essential for me that my garden is an ecosystem – rather than just a production facility for my benefit. And my enjoyment is enhanced greatly by coming across interesting creatures as I garden – the slow worms on my compost heap and dragonflies hovering over my pond for example. Let's look at some of the issues and explore how we can ensure that our gardening is good for the Earth.

Obtaining Plants

As mentioned, plants sold by large garden centres can come with a high carbon footprint and may well have been treated with chemicals that you won't want in your garden. Unbelievably, some plants labelled as pollinator-friendly have been shown to have been treated with pesticides while they are grown in the nurseries, residues of which may kill any pollinators they attract. It's safer to use smaller local nurseries that propagate and grow their own plants, but in any case always check what plants may have been treated with.

Better still is to swap plants with friends and neighbours, buy from plant stalls (such as your local horticultural society or a gardening club might run) or propagate your own via cuttings, division and seeds.

Seeds

There are many benefits of saving your own seeds including: saving money, maintaining genetic diversity, choosing the crops that grow the best and/or taste the best with your particular soil/climate and being able to share seeds with your neighbours.

Many plants go to seed a couple of months after they have flowered, so if the flower is the part you harvest (broccoli, for example) leave one or two plants to fully flower and produce seed in the autumn. Most seeds need to be dried properly, without being exposed to excessive heat, in order to be stored for long periods. Always collect seeds on a dry day and then leave them (or the flower heads) for a couple of weeks, spread out on paper in trays or open boxes, in a dry place indoors. Once they have fully dried, separate the seeds from the flower heads and any chaff (pieces of plant material that were collected inadvertently along with the seeds). Store the seeds in labelled paper envelopes or bags, somewhere cool and dry (a garage, for example) or in an airtight container in the fridge.

With fruiting plants such as tomatoes, apples, peppers, pumpkins and other squashes, the seeds will need to be separated from the flesh of the fruit and washed before being dried on kitchen paper. For those that produce pods, such as beans and peas, wait until the pods are dry and brittle on the plant before collecting them and removing the seeds for further drying indoors. If you grow plants that produce tubers such as potatoes, remember to save enough perfect specimens for planting the following year.

Organic Principles

To grow organically means to use no chemical pesticides, herbicides, fungicides or artificial fertilisers. Furthermore, organic crops should not be genetically modified (GM), radiated or processed with chemicals in any way. Growing organically should go hand-in-hand with aims to lower our carbon footprints and care for the Earth: using sustainable methods, reusing materials or using recycled products, improving biodiversity, using as little packaging as possible and as little fossil fuel energy as possible (ideally none).

Soil Fertility

Other than carbon dioxide and oxygen from the atmosphere, and energy from the sun, plants get everything they need for growth from the soil, including water and nutrients. Organic methods involve ensuring that the soil is healthy, water-retentive and replenished with nutrients naturally. Almost all soils, whether sand, loam or clay, will benefit from increased amounts of organic matter such as home-made compost.

All gardens should have a compost heap or container, however small. To throw away your kitchen waste, weeds, grass-mowings and so on, is to throw away valuable fertility. There are numerous composting bins, cages, tumblers and containers available, many of which are suitable for small plots, but it's better to make your own if you can, using old pallets or other reused materials. If you have the space, the ideal is to create two or three bins or bays so that one is the freshest you are adding new material to, while the others are rotting down.

One key aspect is the mix of materials added. Many garden heaps are made up largely of grass-mowings, weeds and kitchen waste, all of which are rich in nitrogen and known as 'greens'. The ideal compost, however, will be produced from a mixture of roughly two-thirds greens and one-third browns. 'Browns' are carbon-rich and could be made up from straw, stems such as spent tomato vines, woodchips, sawdust, torn-up cardboard and shredded paper. Add these in layers with your green material as you build the heap up, and if it is too dry, water with rainwater before covering the heap with something like a piece of old carpet to add some insulation and stop it drying out.

Other organic methods for improving soil fertility include using leaf mould, plant teas (made from nettles or comfrey for example), mulching, growing green manures (plants, like clover, grown to improve fertility and add organic matter to the soil) and crop rotation.

Growing and Storing Food

Ever since I started growing things I could eat, I have dreamt of living off the land, being self-reliant, living the good life and maybe even going off-grid. However, depending on how much land and time you have available, it needn't be a dream.

Diet also plays a factor; if you just eat fruit and vegetables then it is easier to grow all you need rather than if you also eat bread, rice, pasta and other grain-based foods. Of course it's possible to grow your own grains too, but this adds levels of complexity and needs more land. For many of us, myself included, the compromise is to be self-sufficient (or partly) in some of our favourite crops, whilst buying in some other essentials that are harder to grow or store or need complicated processing.

Storage is a key feature of self-sufficiency as many crops are only harvested at certain times of the year. There are various techniques that enable you to keep or preserve them to last throughout the year, some of which have been used by our ancestors for hundreds or even thousands of years, such as drying, fermenting, making jams and jellies, salting, bottling and pickling. More recently we also have appliances that can help such as freezers, vacuum-packing machines and electric dehydrators.

Dealing with Weeds and Pests

A weed is any plant growing where you don't want it – whether it's an oak tree, a rose bush or a dandelion. There are a certain number of plants that we have been conditioned to think of as always being weeds: thistles, brambles, stinging nettles, and so on. However, all of these are hugely important to wildlife (and can be to us, too): thistles produce attractive flowers – good for butterflies and many other pollinating insects; brambles produce blackberries – good for us and many bird species; nettles can be used to make tea, ease arthritis, or be fermented to create a plant-food; and dandelions have many health benefits as well as attracting numerous beneficial insects.

So before you pull up something that triggers your weeding reflex, ask yourself whether it is doing any damage where it is, or whether it is truly in the way. If not, maybe it can stay there a little longer and do some good (attracting insects and acting as a green manure, for example).

A pest can be defined as an animal that is detrimental to humans or human concerns. In the garden, the most common ones are slugs and snails, aphids (blackfly and greenfly being the most prolific) and the caterpillars of large white and small white butterflies (often collectively called cabbage white butterflies). In the spring, in some areas, wood pigeons can also be a nuisance – eating young brassica plants in particular. Fruits can also be devoured by a number of different birds and some rodents.

The problem with chemical pesticides is that they kill the beneficial predators as well as the pests (upon which they prey). Classic examples include the larvae of ladybirds, hoverflies and lacewings, which devour aphids, yet are equally as susceptible to most pesticides as the aphids themselves. Without these predators in our landscape, pests like aphids, which breed very rapidly, can quickly get a hold and damage crops. With a healthy ecosystem there will always be a balance, however, with predators keeping their prey under control.

So the most effective, environmentally-friendly and least time-consuming method of pest control is simply to ensure that your garden is as wildlife-rich as possible. Here are some examples of the types of predators you want to attract: bats, beetles and centipedes, birds, frogs and toads, hedgehogs, ladybirds, hoverflies and lacewings, newts and slow worms.

It's easy and fun (for children too) to create gardens that attract wildlife. There are a number of additions to your garden, which will not only encourage beneficial animals, but also make your garden more attractive and interesting. Priorities would be:

- Pond(s) with easy access for small animals and shallow areas, marginal plants but no fish (which eat the eggs and young of amphibians and insects)

- A wild patch with long grasses and nettles

- A wildflower area

- Piles of logs, stones, leaves, hedge trimmings etc.

- Insect hotels, bird boxes and bat boxes

If you do need to keep pests away from prized plants and vegetables there are numerous kind ways to do this such as using barriers, netting, cloches, relocating (snails for example) and using companion plants (which can either repel certain pests or lure them away from the plants you want to protect).

Permaculture

Permaculture is an innovative framework for creating sustainable ways of living; a practical method for developing ecologically harmonious, efficient and productive systems that can be used by anyone, anywhere.

Originally derived from the term 'permanent agriculture' (or 'permanent culture'), it is often associated with ways of growing crops that are more sustainable and environmentally friendly. However, as the description above suggests, it is much more holistic than that. Permaculture provides ethics and tools for creating and designing ways of life that are not only sustainable but regenerative, to repair and revitalise our damaged planet. It can apply to how we design our homes, livelihoods, communities, technologies and economies. Permaculture provides co-operative systems which support living ethically in symbiosis with, and in stewardship of, the Earth.

The ethics of permaculture focus on:

- **Earth Care:** Living/gardening in a way that leaves no waste or damage, but regenerates the earth (for example, by using growing techniques such as no-dig methods, mulching, not using chemicals)

- **People Care:** Nurturing yourself and all other people (for example, by ensuring that anything we buy does not involve slavery, child labour or other forms of exploitation)

- **Fair Shares:** Not consuming more than we need and redistributing surplus (for example, giving excess crops to neighbours or food banks).

Although permaculture has been around for a long time now, interest continues to grow and, if you want to learn more, there are many courses held all over the world. The Permaculture Association is a good place to find out about these.

Conclusion

The way of the gardener has become not just something I do, but something I am. It is being engaged with life in a creative way, with many physical and mental benefits. Seeing green and growing things reduces my anxiety and gives me hope. The practical activity of gardening puts me in touch with the Earth on a daily basis. One day I may only have the strength to look after one small plant in a pot on my windowsill, but it will still be the way of the gardener.

* * *

Editor's Note

For further reading, *The Vegan Cook & Gardener: Growing, storing and cooking delicious healthy food all year round*, by Piers Warren and Ella Bee Glendining (Permanent Publications, 2018) is highly recommended.

6
The Way of Contemplation

Chris Holmes

A poor life this if, full of care,
We have no time to stand and stare.
~ Closing lines of *Leisure* by William Henry Davies

I must live above all in the present.
~ Henry David Thoreau

The highest ecstasy is attention at its fullest.
~ Simone Weil

Introduction

When I was in my teens I purchased a book on Medieval history, the front cover of which depicted a monk quietly reading from the Bible. As an adolescent seeking some meaning to life, I was very drawn to this image and its associations – silence, stillness, study, solitude. I instinctively knew that such a life was not for me but there was something there which was very attractive – and if all else failed then it was an option! The attraction has waxed and waned over the years though in a very different form.

Throughout my life I have attended retreats, some silent ones, but mostly with a focus – poetry, music, justice and peace, bodywork, ecological – at monastic communities, friaries and retreat houses. Thomas Merton talked of 'contemplatives in action'; I was more an active person with contemplative habits, a 'part-time contemplative', who enjoyed being in contemplative places with contemplative people but without any desire for total commitment. I believe there are many of us who fall into this category.

I once believed that contemplation and action were in opposition, and indeed they can be if each is distorted, taken to extremes. The contemplative path can turn into escapism, spiritual bypassing and a false bliss while the active path can become a frenzied and mindless thrill seeking. Over time I came to understand that they are complementary, that they are intertwined, yin and yang. The contemplative lifestyle, which makes time in everyday life for quiet, stillness and reflection does not mean letting the issues of the world pass beneath our notice. It means drawing on the resources of contemplation to make a mature response to the world.

The contemplative way is, however, not just a subsidiary of action, needing justification. It may seem to be unproductive, and it is by conventional standards. Our culture sets great store by growth but the contemplative process seems to take us in the opposite direction, towards an inner and outer simplicity. The way of contemplation has a value in itself, a way of being which has a different rhythm, which puts us back in touch with our intrinsic worth and with the worth of all things. Such experience is fundamental to a green spirituality.

Some Basics in the Way of Contemplation

We live in a restless, hyperactive society where busyness, competition and achievement dominate. While there is a vibrant counter-culture (the 'slow' movement that encourages a thoughtful life and the many varieties of spirituality), capitalist socio-economic structures and values are powerful and insidious. Finding time to truly be present to ourselves, when we are free to just appreciate the giftedness of life, when life can be known more as an art than as a task, is not easy.

Slowing down, solitude, silence and attention in the great contemplative traditions seem to be the basic constituents and, in some respects, are practices that are essentially simple to do. However, being able to incorporate these into one's daily living depends upon the circumstances of our life. For many, slowing down and finding any sort of silence and solitude may be very challenging, and giving focused attention may be the last thing needed after an exhausting day. Even if these experiences are possible at a practical level, they can still be painful, particularly at first, for each can access some of our deepest fears and wounds. Fortunately we also have the capacity to deal with them and move on, which may take time and help from a spiritual friend (not necessarily human) or a reputable experienced practitioner.

One area which needs a little more consideration is attention, in my experience the most difficult of all. The practice of attention is fundamental to the contemplative way. For those with a green orientation it means developing a self-forgetful attentiveness to creation that draws us out of our mental preoccupations, learning to perceive and respond to what Wordsworth called 'the life of things'. This 'directed' attention, immersing ourself in Nature, entering into the consciousness of the other-than-human can be hard to attain and sustain, but trying may be one of the most important contributions we can make to ecological renewal and our spiritual life.

In contrast to 'directed' attention, in the natural world our senses are often grabbed by something. The sight and sound of swans flying overhead, the shape of a particular tree, the view as one turns a bend on a mountain path – the attention required ('reflexive' attention) is well nigh effortless. The green contemplative will rejoice in both modes of attention; we are truly blessed.

Contemplative Practices

The contemplative way is sometimes conflated with contemplative practices of which there are many, ancient and modern. These practices are not the whole story, but they are important in so far as they support, enhance and give depth and variety to the spiritual journey. The list of practices is a long one and an online search will reveal an extraordinary range from all parts of the world, from all faiths and none. Many kinds of meditation and prayer, slow reading (*lectio divina*), journaling, varieties of slow movement and bodywork, creative arts and play – all these variations and practitioners, make up an amazing collection of spiritual inspiration and influential forces for transformation.

Practices may be therapeutic and instrumental in orientation and intent, associated with respite, stress relief and improved well-being, both mental and physical. They may also be integral to a more profound personal and communal transformation which is often but not always part of a faith tradition. When the practice takes place in a natural environment, it is my experience that the benefits to well-being are markedly enhanced. In my own green contemplative path, I have found that meditation on the move – slow running and walking in Nature – best suits my disposition. Occasionally the experience is deepened through the poetry of John Clare, surely our greatest Nature poet.

There are many who find the contemplative path difficult through life circumstances and lack the time, space and energy required. I was once in this position and found that the 'power pause', taking five minutes out a couple of times each day for quiet meditation was very helpful. I would often use something from the natural world as a focus, occasionally the image of the Earth taken from space. These things gave much needed perspective and context to the day's activities and helped create an alternative and a more profound rhythm to life. Even when things feel utterly overwhelming it is still good policy to just ‘turn up’ and do those few minutes, even if nothing may appear to happen, and hand over responsibility to the Divine.

The Possibility of Transformation

Slowing, solitude, silence, attention and contemplative practice are necessary, but there is more. This is the desire to make a change in one’s way of life, to undergo some sort of transformation towards, as already indicated, an inner and outer simplicity. For those following a path of green spirituality (which may or may not involve a relationship with the Divine) it will mean making connections, rejoicing in the interdependence of things, delighting in the forms and images of creation and immersing oneself in the greater whole of Nature. It means re-membering and recovering the ‘Original Blessing’, an Earth of extraordinary diversity, complexity and beauty, despite humanity’s perverse actions to wreck its own home.

The Earth itself is part of something much greater. “The Universe is the primary revelation of the Divine, the primary scripture, the primary locus of divine-human communication” (Thomas Berry). We can glimpse this reality in the night sky, a source of awe and wonder, leading one to ponder – and somehow feel – the mystery and immensity of the Cosmos. Sadly, the majesty of the night sky is rare to behold in south east England, but thankfully very much available in other parts of the world. When I was a child in the 1950s there seemed to be many more stars than in the present day and I grieve that my grandchildren miss out on this revelation.

There is a beauty in the heavens but nothing, as far as we know, to compare with the beauty of Earth and the amazing variety of its creatures. Paying real and deep attention to our other-than-human kin seems a fundamental requirement in our contemplative practice and transformation. The human way of being only makes sense if it is woven into the countless other ways of being alive with the animals, plants and ecosystems all around us. If we can also reconnect with our own animal nature, as a rich heritage to be welcomed, then we might accept more easily our common destiny with the rest of living beings.

Connecting with our animal nature leads me to consider the inner journey. In practice I often find that I cannot distinguish between the outer and inner, they are so intertwined. Approaching 80 years on this Earth, I still feel a relative beginner, particularly as I survey all of the wisdom that has gone before and all that is present now. I have been very struck by the similarities between the Christian contemplative tradition, in particular the Desert Fathers and Mothers of the 3rd and 4th centuries, and the modern psychoanalytic tradition. This was brilliantly drawn out in *Soul Making*, written well over 30 years ago by the late Alan Jones, an Episcopal priest. This book, which excites and inspires me to this day, shows how the inner journey can take one to some fearsome places, personal and communal, places visited by many others over the centuries. It also shows how our deep sorrow and despair about the state of the Earth and humanity is far from just a modern experience. We may find some solace in the ancient desert practice of the Gift of Tears, an expression not simply of personal loss but a part of a restorative spiritual practice that can awaken us to the bonds that connect us to each other and to the larger ecological whole.

The way of contemplation has many other guides for the inner journey which can lead us not only into darkness but also into a resilience and the ability to face up to the ecological catastrophes of our time.

Benefits of the Way of Contemplation

I feel uncomfortable using the word 'benefits'. The contemplative way can deteriorate into the search for spiritual acquisition and rewards, competitiveness, self-delusion, sloth and a puritanical 'holier than thou' attitude. I am all too aware of some of these urges in myself, as well as in others. Intercessory prayer is not a feature of my practice but sometimes I ask for Divine help to lead me through the tortuous and labyrinthine ways of my mind. We never graduate beyond needing help.

However, being human seems to require some sense of context and that one is moving on. Therefore, I would suggest three main benefits:

> First, feeling part of a great tradition. There are extraordinary riches to be found within the contemplative traditions of the world and it is a consolation to know that countless individuals and communities have trodden this path before. These may be hard times but surely we are blessed by the quantity and availability of

wisdom from past contemplatives. I wonder what the contemplatives in two or three centuries will make of our preoccupations!

Second, there is a wonderful worldwide community of contemplative green spirits and no lack of options when it comes to choosing an affiliation. I am often told that many monasteries and retreat houses are struggling to stay afloat. However, dispersed communities and small groups are alive and well; the Internet has been an extraordinary instrument in revival.

Third, the contemplative path can, paradoxically, make one a more grounded person yet also open us up to experiencing and somehow feeling in our body the big important dimensions of life. The biggest dimension is perhaps our own demise, which for myself and many friends is surely on the horizon. Meditating upon this is surely an integral part of the way of contemplation, even though there is so much around us and in the media. Being sensitive to the cycle of life and death, to the cycle of the seasons and to our extraordinary Earth history – 'deep time' – gives context and consolation to our walk into darkness.

If one completes the journey to one's own heart,
one will find oneself in the heart of everyone else.
~ Thomas Keating

* * *

Further Reading

Douglas Christie, *The Blue Sapphire of the Mind: Notes for a Contemplative Ecology*. Oxford University Press, 2012.

Brian Draper and Howard Green, *Soulful Nature*. Canterbury Press, 2020.

Martin Laird, *Into the Silent Land. The Practice of Contemplation*. Darton Longman and Todd, 2006.

Henry David Thoreau, *Walden*. New Morla Editions, 2024.

7
The Way of Community

Hilary Norton

Never doubt that a small group of thoughtful committed citizens can change the world: indeed, it's the only thing that ever has.
~ Margaret Mead

Communities are groups of people who share something in common, such as a place, interests, or identity, and often feel a sense of belonging. People can be part of many communities at the same time and may also come and go from communities.

Experiencing a sense of belonging is vital for our psychological well-being. Being a part of a healthy community can help us feel connected to others, as well as feel we are part of something larger than ourselves. This is especially important for people who've experienced loss, or who are feeling isolated, marginalized or bullied.

Being a part of a healthy community can also provide

us with support. When we're going through a difficult time, it can be enormously helpful to have people to whom we can turn to share our stresses. Community members can offer us emotional support, practical help, and advice. They can also help us to feel we aren't alone in our struggles.

A community can also help us to develop a sense of identity. When we're part of a community, we often have shared values and beliefs. We feel connected to our history and culture. This can help us feel we have a place in the world. Research shows that people who are involved in strong communities tend to be healthier and are more likely to exercise regularly and eat healthily.

Many GreenSpirit people are members of other groups that mean a lot to them, such as walking groups, parent-teacher groups, development groups, gardening groups, storytelling groups, prison visiting groups, music making groups as well as belonging to GreenSpirit and taking part in its activities.

GreenSpirits have an extra reason to join in community. Most of us believe that all things and beings are interconnected, and that collaborative action will serve the whole. This belief comes from the holistic principle of "undivided wholeness" with the idea that everything is in a state of process or becoming. The mystics of most wisdom traditions tell us that "We are One". In GreenSpirit, and some of our other groups, we belong to a social movement that awakens us to our interconnectedness, encouraging a critical mass of collaborative action serving the good of the whole.

We describe GreenSpirit as "a network of people who

practise loving our living planet". And within our network we have a criss-cross of small communities that have grown together over the years. Many of us meet regularly, face to face and online e.g. in local GreenSpirit groups to celebrate the seasons, like harvest, and festivals like the Solstices. Many of us meet regularly from different parts of the country at our national events and online, weekly or monthly. These days in which we live present us with challenges that are often met more easily when we have others around us.

GreenSpirit has a management committee, the trustees, responsible for the running of the charity. In between our termly business meetings we meet monthly for connection and sharing. We always start our meetings with meditation, aware that we want our decisions and actions to be heart-centred and inspired.

GreenSpirit brings people together in various ways, locally and nationally. At our Annual Gatherings, which are in-person events, we have brought in speakers and teachers to inspire and stimulate us. Over the course of 30 years we have had a large variety of speakers. We have done work out of doors with Glennie Kindred on the theme of "Living at the Wild Edges" at EarthSpirit in Glastonbury and listened to other speakers such as Philip Carr-Gomm, and Alan Heeks considering our relationships with trees, made shamanic talismans from different sorts of wood and crafted talking sticks and dream-catchers. We have heard from architects like Herbert Giradet about greening cities, physicists like Jude Currivan telling us about the Universe,

Gaia and Us, and the holomovement, authors like Lyndsey Clark about imagination and how important it is. We've learned about Earth and living systems from scientists like Chris Clarke, Stephan Harding, Brian Swimme, Rupert Sheldrake and David Abram amongst others. And musicians Nigel Shaw and Carolyn Hillyer helped us to celebrate the Threshold of Winter at a Samhain gathering.

We always spend time meditating together, singing and being creative, as well as listening and mulling over fascinating topics. Annual Gatherings are a great way to come together each year and absorb something that inspires and challenges us. An example of an inspiring talk at an Annual Gathering I'd like to share is when Alastair McIntosh, author of Spiritual Activism: Leadership as Service told us a story from the Hindu sacred text, the Bhagavad Gita, in which an ancient battle provides a metaphor for our inner conflicts, and what it means to let our lives be held in prayer.

The Penguin Classics' translation renders the Gita's opening line: "On the field of Truth, on the battlefield of life, what came to pass, Sanjaya...?" This is speaking metaphorically about three levels of reality: "On the field of Truth (1), on the battlefield of life (2), what came to pass (3), Sanjaya?", verse 1:1.

Sanjaya is the eagle-eyed charioteer to the blind king who lacks vision without spiritual eyes. Sanjaya calls out to the blind king to tell him what is up ahead. And through his blow-by-blow account of that which came to pass, Sanjaya draws the reader, to the attitude of prayer. The Bhagavad

Gita calls us to be aware of what is present and comes into being for this is nested in the "battlefield" that is our life on Earth. And this in turn is nested in the Way and the Truth, by which each level of our being rests in mystery. We learned the lesson of spiritual activism, that we need to speak our truth to the politicians and leaders of our time.

GreenSpirit annual Wild Weeks are retreats in Snowdonia at Cae Mabon, a faery-land settlement in North Wales with Snowdon nearby. This place gives itself to us elementally, here we can very easily connect with the elements we are made of.

Cae Mabon has a family of beautiful, natural, earthy structures that provide appealing spaces for us to sleep, meet, retreat, work and play. GreenSpirit has been going there since the mid-90s. Cae Mabon is at the foot of mountains with breath-taking views, in an unspoiled oak wood beside a rushing stream and a deep lake. The Wild Week is a lovely way to focus on the other-than-human, the elements, the wind, the water, the fire and earth. We connect, in the liminal spaces, where the elements meet. We eat together, sit around the fire in fellowship, swim in the lake, climb the hills, and join together drumming and storytelling in the thatched roundhouse, a true somatic connection with the elements. We make ritual together held in the folds of Nature's beauty. The owner of Cae Mabon in Wales is a long-time GreenSpirit member and has shared his wonderful stories and songs at our Annual Gatherings as well as on our Wild Weeks.

Our Walking Breaks are particularly enjoyed for being

more casual times spent with others in beautiful parts of the countryside that uplift our spirits. Connecting this way with the natural world is especially enriching for those of us who live in cities and built-up areas of bricks and concrete. The Walking Break naturally lends itself to being an Earth-centred time of honouring Nature and our interrelationship with all living things, where we share poems, stories or simply stand quietly in awe of the beauty of our planet home and feel love for Earth and the abundant array of life. We now have guided walks for striders, strollers and stragglers as we have found this suits more people. We also have evenings of sharing craft/art/stories/songs and some devotional activities.

As GreenSpirit has changed over the past 30 years, peoples' reasons for gathering together in community have changed. Before the start of the new millennium, many of us in faith groups were aware that some sections of society were marginalised in the groups we belonged to. Many felt wounded because of prejudice against women, gays and lesbians, and because of racial differences. In those early years the Association for Creation Spirituality (the former name of GreenSpirit) was active in bringing about healing situations where folks felt accepted for who they were, not judged because of sexuality, race, gender, or for other reasons. Our wild weeks had an "Honouring the Goddess/Feminine" focus. As wounds healed and as we identified more with Gaia, the charity was formed and re-named and the regular seasonal festivals were celebrated by local groups, demonstrating our closer connection to the Earth. We also, at the time, listened to Thomas Berry, Brian Swimme, Joanna Macy and others and became even more aware of our interconnectedness with the whole of Creation. So, for us, the Earth community includes the other-than-humans living on this planet with us: the trees, creatures, the waters, the mountains and plants.

We have had many very inspiring members over the years who have been involved in giving talks, running events, creating publications, organising celebrations, running a book service, publishing books, inspiring connection and facilitating communication. Our community continues to grow in maturity as well as numbers.

Online Activities

In spring 2020, events had to be done online because of the pandemic, and GreenSpirit has continued with these online activities and added to them, which has expanded the reach of our activities and therefore our community.

We started holding seasonal celebrations online following the Celtic and the solar calendar. We are joined by a collection of lovely people from all over the UK and sometimes from America and Europe. The format of our celebrations allows for contributions from anybody who wants to bring something and this sharing allows us to connect more deeply with each other.

We now have new friends in various parts of the UK and overseas who we are drawing close to because of meeting regularly (weekly) online at a deep spiritual level. During the pandemic we ran some Wisdom Keeper Groups where we talked about the future we want to bring about and re-enchanting the world. These meetings morphed into our two Anam Cara groups, one weekly evening and one daytime twice monthly.

In the weekly online Anam Cara meetings up to twelve of us come together to share, meditate and talk about various aspects of the spiritual life. Topics include: presence, distraction, our legacy, good versus evil, important values, significant times in our lives, death and the lessons we have learned through the people and events we have encountered. Through this we have developed a deep level of sharing and fondness for each other, as well as trust and love. The daytime Anam Cara is twice monthly and is a slightly smaller group. It follows the same format and our heart-felt connections are deepening because of regular sharing.

The benefits of coming together in a GreenSpirit community supports finding out who we really are (personally) in relationship to others. These groups can be places of spiritual growth and maturing. The GreenSpirit council (the trustees) and the Anam Cara groups, and other groups we belong to are all places where we can find out about ourselves and our interrelationship with others.

In GreenSpirit we want to be the best human beings we can be, so we want to know ourselves as well as possible. In the communities we belong to, we open to closer relationships and can more easily see ourselves through the eyes of others. If something is said or happens that causes an adverse reaction (maybe hurt or anger) or triggers us, we can take a moment of calm reflection and find out what is happening within. It may be solved simply with a conversation, or an apology, or it may be a more deeply held wound surfacing that we will need to spend more time on or seek help for. The healing of our wounds will help us to be alongside other people and build our capacity for bringing healing to others and the planet. I feel this is what we are called to in this time of harmful values and broken lives.

Our closer relationships help with co-regulation (a process that helps people develop the ability to self-regulate) which is important for healthy functioning. Co-regulation is especially important for young people, but it can be used by anyone to learn to self-regulate and take a more aware place in the world, and thus better able to support others.

Through regulating how we are with others, we become more mature adults, which means empathising and being with other people, deeply listening to each other without judgment and acknowledging each other and supporting the healing of any deep wounds relating to our differences.

In a world rife with polarisation and focus on differences we need humans who are able to find their calm centre and join empathetically with others, who can use non-violent communication, and respond in love. If (or maybe I should write "when" since we already see it) society starts breaking down due to climate change, increasing wars, increasing flood risks, increasing refugees, and financial instability we will need these skills.

It may seem odd that a chapter on community should include this following quote from Blaise Pascal, "All men's miseries derive from not being able to sit quiet in a room alone", but the ability to find calm and peace within is one of the most important contributions to building a meaningful and fulfilling community.

This quotation below by John O'Donohue describes how aloneness will lead to the oneness of community and true belonging:

> *Each one of us is alone in the world. It takes great courage to meet the full force of your aloneness. Most of the activity in society is subconsciously designed to quell the voice crying in the wilderness within you. The mystic Thomas à Kempis said that when you go out into the world, you return having lost some of yourself. Until you learn to inhabit your aloneness, the lonely distraction and noise of society will seduce you into false belonging, with which you will only become empty and weary. When you face your aloneness, something begins to happen. Gradually, the sense of bleakness changes into a sense of true belonging. This is a slow and open-ended transition but it is utterly vital in order to come into rhythm with your own individuality. In a sense this is the endless task of finding your true home within your life. It is not narcissistic, for as soon as you rest in the house of your own heart, doors and windows begin to open outwards to the world. No longer on the run from your aloneness, your connections with others become real and creative. You no longer need to covertly scrape affirmation from others or from projects outside yourself. This is slow work; it takes years to bring your mind home.*
>
> ~ Excerpt from *Eternal Echoes*
> by John O'Donohue, HarperCollins, 1998.

There is an evolutionary impulse to unite in compassion and action working together for the betterment of all. It is a call to unity, and community.

Our evolution and our inherent potential depend upon the dynamic co-evolutionary partnerships we're nurturing in GreenSpirit in these unprecedented times. We are invited to participate in catalysing a social movement to balance and harmonize our relationship with each other, the planet and Cosmos. This is why I feel I am here on the planet at this time.

> *The only way forward is for people to bind themselves closer together than ever before. The glue that will bind us has to be our common tenderness of heart. If we learn how to cultivate tsewa,[1] we can see each other as members of a large, wonderful extended family. With that view, our diversity will only be an advantage, an aid to our individual and collective growth. It will give us more to embrace, more occasions for opening our hearts.*
>
> ~ Dzigar Kongtrul

* * *

1. *Tsewa* is the Tibetan word for an innate tenderness of the heart.

Further Reading

Thomas Hübl,
Attuned: Practicing Interdependence to Heal Our Trauma – and Our World,
Sounds True, 2023

Terry Pattern (foreword by Andrew Harvey),
A New Republic of the Heart: An Ethos for Revolutionaries.
North Atlantic Books, 2018.

8
The Way of Activism

Two Perspectives

...one has a moral responsibility to disobey unjust laws.
~ Martin Luther King Jr

I've learnt that no one is too small to make a difference...
The real power belongs to the people...
All we have to do is to wake up and change.
~ Greta Thunberg

Piers Warren: Practical Suggestions

We have much to be concerned about regarding the health of the planet these days. The climate crisis is the big one of course but is intertwined with many other problems such as population growth, pollution, land and water use, food waste, habitat destruction, a growing global demand for meat, soil contamination, exploitation of marine resources and so on. It's easy to become overwhelmed by these huge topics and climate anxiety is a real and growing issue. But taking steps to become part of the solution rather than the problem, and encouraging others to do the same, can really help to give us hope, reduce anxiety, and make a difference.

An activist is someone who campaigns to bring about political and social change and this can take many forms. Matthew Fox, who has highlighted and expanded upon the tradition of Creation Spirituality since the 1970s, describes how an activist is a contemporary term that has links with some of the early prophets, as being a prophet in early biblical times often meant someone who stood up for and took action against injustice, the oppressed and marginalised.

Let's explore some of the ways of the Earth-centred activist so you can decide what you feel most comfortable doing.

Lifestyle Choices

Some of us may be activists without even realising it by living in an environmentally friendly way and by setting an example for others. In addition, the choices you make will send a message to suppliers, industry and politicians that there is demand for a kinder way of living. Consuming less is of course the most Earth-centred way of living your life but there are some necessities. Here are some examples of choices that can be made with the planet in mind:

- renewable energy providers
- ethical banking
- eating less or no meat and dairy

- gardening organically
- stop flying and use public transport or walk and cycle more
- reduce water usage and wastage
- plant trees
- insulate your house
- grow your own food
- use borrowing schemes for things like tools rather than buying new
- repair things rather than replace
- work from home more
- avoid seasonal excesses such as buying food from other parts of the world because they are not in season where you live

These and others are explored in more detail on my Green Action Toolkit webpage on GreenSpirit's website.

Research and Educate

In order to spread the word as an activist we need to have our facts straight. The Internet has made research a lot easier and quicker but we need to be careful where we get our information. Explore the areas that interest you most and use sources that use evidence-based science. For example, if the decline in bird populations is of concern to you, and an area where you would like to be an activist for change, then a good starting point would be to look at the BTO (British Trust for Ornithology) and the RSPB (Royal Society for the Protection of Birds), both of which employ and undertake science-based surveys and activities to get the most accurate and up-to-date data that can be presented to politicians, land-owners and other decision-makers. Organisations like these can also tell you how you can help them as an activist.

Social Media

Billions of people around the world use social media platforms these days, such as Facebook, X, Instagram, YouTube, WhatsApp, and TikTok, to spread the word about issues they are concerned about. Using them can be a very quick and effective way to reach large numbers of people, and usually at no cost. It's a useful way of distributing petitions, news of demonstrations, and information that may affect the choices people make when it comes to their lifestyle, what organisations to support, who to vote for and so on. But as there is little censorship on these platforms you do need to be careful who you listen to as misinformed conspiracy theories abound. Always check science-based evidence and use common sense.

Art/Photography/Film

We are all creative in one way or another and using our creations can be an effective means of activism. With advances in technology and ubiquitous smartphones, it is easier than ever to take photos (including ones of your artwork) and short films which can carry a punchy message. It has been shown that people are more likely to pay attention to a visual image than read a paragraph of text.

Longer films generally need TV or cinema dissemination and promotional budgets, but with your own camera or phone it is relatively easy to make short campaign films, host them on a platform like YouTube (at no cost) and then spread the word via social media.

Writing

Whether it is for books, magazines, blogs or social media posts, we can all use writing as a means of activism. As before, make sure your research is clearly focused and factual. If you have special areas of interest there are likely to be relevant magazines that are worth approaching about proposed articles. Setting up your own blog online is usually free, the overall aim is to build a following using social media.

Giving Talks

If you have the courage, skills and enough passion to do a bit of public speaking, giving talks is an excellent way to spread the word. There are many special interest groups which meet regularly and are often on the lookout for new speakers; local horticultural societies and women's groups for example, and you'll usually get paid too. A talk of about an hour is a good length to start with. And if you can illustrate it with images and information using presentation software like PowerPoint or Keynote you will find it easier to deliver and more engaging for the audience. Think carefully about the approach and title of your talk so that people aren't put off before you start or feel they will be hectored. For example, a guide to local butterflies and moths will be an attractive talk and along the way, you can talk about the decline in insects and what can be done about it.

Supporting Charities/Organisations/Groups

By joining a charity or supporting an NGO (Non-Governmental Organisation) in an area that interests you, you will be giving them more power and influence whilst gaining more information that you can use in other ways. Many groups also have numerous ways that you can help them on the activism front whether that be attending rallies, fund-raising, hands-on volunteering (conservation work on the land, for example), leafleting, promoting petitions and so on. Use the Internet to find organisations that you would like to get involved with ¬– if you are concerned about marine pollution and overfishing for example, the Marine Conservation Society would be a great place to start.

Using Your Vote and Your MP

Many of the change-making decisions relating to the big topics like climate change, transport, what public money is spent on etc. are made by politicians. Increasingly, at each election, topics are debated ahead so that voters can make appropriate choices. If climate change is your biggest concern this may well influence your vote and it'll be fairly easy to work out which political party is likely to make the most difference. Whether or not you get the MP of your choice, it is worth contacting them regularly (often email is the easiest way) to let them know of your priorities and concerns.

*

Ian Mowll: Practical Activism

Being the change I want to see in the world is, for me, is an essential part of my spiritual journey. Otherwise, my spirituality is 'just an idea' without grounded reality.

I've always been drawn to campaigning because many of the differences I want to see in the world need to be done on a society-wide basis. For instance, offshore wind-farms could make a big difference in sustainable energy, which needs to be done by companies supported by the Government.

To my surprise, campaigning and its associated activism have been a lot of fun for several reasons: I meet likeminded people, so I feel affirmed in what I am doing, I feel part of a wider movement, and it gives me an appropriate channel for my anger about the eco-injustices in the world.

I joined Extinction Rebellion in 2019 when the movement galvanised a whole wave of optimism that the carbon emissions tide could be turned. This honeymoon period was a wonderful example of rapid, decentralised collaboration with non-violence at its core. Even the police were at first friendly towards the movement. Almost inevitably, this did not last as Extinction Rebellion actions became more focussed and consequently the police less tolerant.

At its outset, local Extinction Rebellion groups quickly

formed, and I joined a local one in Newham, East London. It was amazing to suddenly meet a group of dedicated and skilled people, some with a good deal of campaigning experience.

One memorable action we took was outside the offices of a multi-national oil company. We arrived early in the morning with our placards and then a group acted out a stop oil routine. This group wore jumpsuits, caps and batons in order to act out the routine used to signal for planes to stop. The effect of a group of people wearing the same clothes and acting out the same routine to music was quite compelling, and it lifted the spirits of us all. There was chanting, and also speeches by some well-known activists. The police were present to ensure order and hardly anyone entered the offices – maybe the company told its employees to stay away for the day, if so, the action had a direct impact. Another memorable event was at the end of a long day's march. There was a mini-festival in one of London's parks and several faith groups were invited to show how their faith tradition inspired them to face the climate crisis with invocations, poems and speeches. At the heart of GreenSpirit is an acceptance of people of all faiths and none. And so, this event was a wonderful example of how different faith traditions can come together with a common focus on the wellbeing of the planet – Nature helped us all to connect.

I was amazed how quickly the new group of people I met in my local Extinction Rebellion group gelled and got on with a lot of actions so easily. We went on marches, had stalls to raise awareness and funds, created direct action protests and had some social events. Perhaps the clarity of what we were trying to achieve helped to bring us together. GreenSpirit, as an organisation, has also been on several climate change marches as it is committed to raising awareness around sustainability.

For me, GreenSpirit is a place where I can meet like-minded people and learn from others how best to make a positive difference. The world is changing rapidly and none of us can keep up with all of the changes. But by coming together and learning from each other, there is a chance that we can make the large-scale impacts which are so vital to the health of our planet and all living beings.

* * *

Further Reading

Chris Packham and Megan McCubbin, *Back to Nature: How to love life – and save it.* Two Roads, 2020.

Extinction Rebellion, *This Is Not A Drill: An Extinction Rebellion Handbook.* Penguin, 2019.

About the Contributors

Richard Adams has a longstanding interest in appropriate technology, education and holistic herbal medicine. He helped to establish Europe's first BSc honours degree in Herbal Medicine. Richard lives and practises Herbal Medicine in London, England. He enjoys hill walking, music making and the theatre.

In response to his heartfelt need to think differently, from his conditioned thinking, about the natural world, he is exploring an Earth-centred consciousness that engages people's hearts and minds, creatively, with Mother Nature. He finds that new values, morals and ethics emerge from such adventures which, in turn, inform his actions in the world.

Richard first came across GreenSpirit in the mid-1990s at St James's Church, Piccadilly, London, when informally researching the life of William Blake. He finds GreenSpirit to be a stimulating and nurturing community that engages with issues relevant to the human and other than human communities.

Chris Holmes's conversion to a green ethos was gradual but thorough. He worked for nearly three decades in the financial markets, and as Director of a large City institution was instrumental in the introduction and development of 'green' investment funds – one of the few activities he feels good about during this period! Since leaving the financial sector in the mid-1990s he has spent his time in voluntary work and developing a range of eco-related interests.

His hobbies include walking, running, tennis, playing guitar, the Christian contemplative tradition and retreat movement, local history and the poetry of John Clare. Chris is married to Jill, also a 'greenspiriter', and lives in Surrey. He has been involved with GreenSpirit for 25 years and on the Council for most of that time. He says: "It is home for me emotionally, intellectually and spiritually. I feel blessed to be part of this movement." He is also involved with the Green Party, Garden Organic, the John Clare Society, the Thomas Merton Society among others.

Marian Van Eyk McCain: Formerly a transpersonal psychotherapist/workshop leader/health educator with an MA in East-West Psychology, Marian officially 'retired' in 1996 to concentrate on her writing. She is the author of two books on women and ageing, two on downshifting/simple living, one on self-therapy, and two works of fiction. In 2010 she edited the anthology *GreenSpirit: Path to a New Consciousness*, and has contributed, both as author and editor, to the GreenSpirit Book Series and *GreenSpirit* magazine. She was a columnist for *Crone Magazine* and editor of the

Elderwoman Newsletter. As well as writing essays and articles on a wide range of subjects, Marian also has a background as a blogger. She started an online social network for elderwomen and enjoyed interacting with network members from around the world. Her other interests are Permaculture, hiking, reading, word games and travel.

Marian lives in rural North Devon with her American partner Sky and spends part of each year in Europe and the USA. They have four children and eight grandchildren. She has been a member of GreenSpirit for many years.

Ian Mowll is GreenSpirit's Coordinator and many people's first point of contact with the organization. It is a role that he loves. He is also one of the editors of *GreenSpirit* magazine and has edited books in the GreenSpirit Book Series.

Ian's career started with computing in the financial markets, followed by charity/social enterprise work and now he is more and more involved in spiritual development. Some of the things he loves to do are: cooking, storytelling, 5Rhythms dancing and having ideas. He lives in Stratford, East London.

Ian has been involved in GreenSpirit since 1999 and sees it as his spiritual home. He says: "Finding GreenSpirit was the first time I found somewhere where I truly felt I could be spiritually 'me' without having to pretend. When joining GreenSpirit, occasionally people use the phrase 'welcome home' – a phrase that feels good to me." He is also involved with the OneSpirit Interfaith Foundation and is an independent celebrant.

Hilary Norton lives in East London. Her four children are grown up but apart from one son in Japan, they live nearby. She is an active grandparent. She loves being in the East End and cycles most places. Hilary believes strongly in making cities greener places to be, so supports the London Wildlife Trust, Woodcraft Folk, sustainable architecture, allotment gardening and other local green initiatives. She sings in, and helps to run, a local community choir.

Hilary has played a key role in GreenSpirit since the mid-1990s. As well as serving on Council, she runs a local GreenSpirit group in Stratford and organises some zoom meetings for GreenSpirit, and in person: both the annual GreenSpirit walking holiday/retreat and Wild Week in Snowdonia.

Piers Warren is an author, conservationist, film-maker, activist, cook and veganic veg-grower living in the UK. He is also a regular features contributor to *GreenSpirit* magazine.

He is well known throughout the wildlife film-making industry as the Principal of WILDEYE – the International School of Wildlife Film-making, which he founded in 1999. With a strong background in biology, education and conservation, he has had a lifelong passion for wildlife films and has a wide knowledge of natural history. He is one of the founders of the international organisation Filmmakers for Conservation and was Vice President for the first three years. Wildeye Publishing have become the leading producers of instructional wildlife film-making books in the world.

Although Piers has written books and many magazine articles on a wide range of subjects, he is also known for writing the highly-acclaimed supernatural thriller *Black Shuck: The Devil's Dog* (shortlisted for the East Anglia Book Awards and Norfolk Magazine's Book of the Month). He is keen to promote organic principles and permaculture techniques, sustainability, veganism and green-thinking. His best-selling books are in these fields including the co-production with his daughter, Ella Bee Glendining, *The Vegan Cook & Gardener*. He has had a passionate interest in self-sufficiency since childhood and currently lives in Sussex where he grows his own food.

Stephen Wollaston was given the name **Santoshan** (contentment) by an English swami in the mid-90s. He is a Psychosynthesis counsellor, OneSpirit Interfaith Foundation minister, professional graphic designer, writer, teacher and musician. He holds a BA honours degree in religious studies and a postgraduate certificate in religious education from King's College London. In the late 70s he was the principal bass guitarist of one of London's first punk rock bands, The Wasps. Additionally, he has helped war refugees and long-term unemployed students with English language skills and was an academic writing coordinator at a medical university in the Middle East for four years.

He is the current Chair of GreenSpirit's Publications Committee, is the main typographic designer of *GreenSpirit* magazine and the GreenSpirit Book Series, and has edited and contributed to titles in the Series. He began writing when a close friend, UK medium Glyn Edwards, asked him to collaborate on an extensive development manual with him. Since then, he has authored, coauthored and edited over a dozen books on different areas of Eastern and Western spirituality, including *Spirituality Unveiled: Awakening to Creative Life*; *Rivers of Green Wisdom: Exploring Christian and Yogic Earth-Centred Spirituality*; and *Realms of Wondrous Gifts: Psychic, Mediumistic and Miraculous Powers in the Great Mystical and Wisdom Traditions*, which assesses different traditions and experiences.

* * *

GreenSpirit Book Series & Other Resources

We at GreenSpirit hope you have enjoyed reading this book and that it has whetted your appetite to read more in our low-cost book series and discover the many and varied ways in which green spirituality can be expressed in every area of our lives and culture. You may also wish to visit our website, which has information about our free for members magazine, GreenSpirit annual events, the benefits of membership and much more: **www.greenspirit.org.uk**

Other titles in the GreenSpirit Book Series

Available in various eBook formats and in paperback and hardback. eBook editions are available for free for members of GreenSpirit.

What is Green Spirituality? Edited by Marian Van Eyk McCain.

All Our Relations: GreenSpirit Connections with the More-than-Human World. Edited by Marian Van Eyk McCain .

The Universe Story in Science and Myth. By Greg Morter and Niamh Brennan.

Rivers of Green Wisdom: Exploring Christian and Yogic Earth-Centred Spirituality. By Santoshan (Stephen Wollaston).

Pathways of Green Wisdom: Discovering Earth-Centred Teachings in Spiritual and Religious Traditions. Edited by Santoshan (Stephen Wollaston).

Deep Green Living. Edited by Marian Van Eyk McCain.

The Rising Water Project: Real Stories of Flooding, Real Stories of Downshifting. Compiled by Ian Mowll.

Dark Nights of the Green Soul: From Darkness to New Horizons. Edited by Ian Mowll and Santoshan (Stephen Wollaston).

Awakening to Earth-Centred Consciousness: Selection from GreenSpirit magazine. Edited by Ian Mowll and Santoshan (Stephen Wollaston).

GreenSpirit Reflections. Compiled by Santoshan (Stephen Wollaston)

Anthology of Poems for GreenSpirits. Compiled by Joan Angus.

The Lilypad List: Seven Steps to the Simple Life. By Marian Van Eyk McCain.

Meditations with Thomas Berry: With additional material by Brian Swimme. Selected by June Raymond.

GreenSpirit

magazine

GreenSpirit magazine is free for members and is published in both print and electronic formats. Each issue includes essential topics connected with Earth-based spirituality. It honours Nature as a great teacher, celebrates the creativity and interrelatedness of all life and the Universe, affirms biodiversity and human differences, and honours the prophetic voice of artists.

'GreenSpirit' presents an ideal view of life with practical application. It is a joyful, inspiring and uplifting read.
~ Satish Kumar

For many of us, it's the spirit running through that limitless span of green organisations and ideas that anchors all the work we do. And 'GreenSpirit' is an invaluable source of insight, information and inspiration.
~ Jonathon Porritt

GreenSpirit

Path to a New Consciousness

Edited by Marian Van Eyk McCain

Only by understanding the Universe as a vast, holistic system and Earth as a unit within it can we help restore balance to that unit.

Only by placing Earth and its ecosystems – about which we now understand so much – at the centre of all our thinking can we avert ecological disaster.

Only by bringing our thinking back into balance with feeling, intuition and awareness and by grounding ourselves in a sense of the sacred in all things can we achieve a new level of consciousness.

Green spirituality is the key to a new, twenty-first century consciousness. And here is the most comprehensive book ever written on green spirituality.

Published by Earth Books

'GreenSpirit: Path to a New Consciousness' offers numerous healing and inspiring insights; notably, that Earth and the universe are primary divine Revelation, a truth to be transmitted to our children as early and effectively as possible.'

~ Thomas Berry (January 2009)

www.ingramcontent.com/pod-product-compliance
Ingram Content Group UK Ltd.
Pitfield, Milton Keynes, MK11 3LW, UK
UKHW040807150425
5480UKWH00013B/123